Josh C. Jones

Making sense of
America's newest
Guild...
Again

What I discovered in my search for answers.

"What if I said..."

FMS
BOOK

MAKING SENSE OF AMERICA'S NEWEST GUILD...AGAIN

Josh C. Jones

What I discovered in my search for answers.

Making sense of America's newest Guild...Again:

What I discovered in my search for answers.

ISBN: 979-8-9870614-0-4 (Paperback)
ISBN: 979-8-9870614-1-1 (Ebook)

First Edition

FMS Books

Cover Art, Editing, Layout and Design by Josh C. Jones.

All opinions expressed in this book are the author's.

DEDICATION

This book is dedicated to everyone who exercised their freedom of speech and individual liberty, ethically and morally, as granted by God and secured by the Constitution of the United States of America.

CONTENTS

ACKNOWLEDGMENTS

"God gave you a gift of 86,400 seconds today. Have you used one to say 'thank you?'"[1]

William Arthur Ward

First and foremost, I would like to thank God. Without Him, I could not do anything, I would not have anything, and I would be lost, wandering blindly in the world, confused about who I am, and be easily deceived by every breath of wind that blows in my ear, being blown in every direction, never stable, and never finding a firm footing in life—a firm foundation.

I would like to thank my parents for loving me and raising me to not only have a strong foundation but to also understand my foundation, and for encouraging my inquisitiveness, which I do believe has helped me grow not only solid and firm, but also understanding.

I thank my brother for always being a shoulder I could lean on; and I thank my sister for encouraging me in my messages and teachings—especially my podcast episodes.

I would like to thank all my friends. We don't always see eye-to-eye. In fact, we don't always believe the same things when it comes to politics, religion, foundations, or life, but we do love each other and value our friendship. For that, I am deeply thankful.

I would also like to thank everyone whom I had the privilege and opportunity to witness in action, whether in person, online, in video, or any other medium by which I was able to calculate and deduce my findings in my search for answers. I would like to thank everyone who I was able to talk with and talk to about MAGA; you all greatly helped with my conclusions in my search for answers. Whether you knew I was talking to you or not, and whether you knew the reason I was talking to you or not, I still thank you for helping me in my search for answers. I also would like to thank all those who called me names, defriended me, tried to lie about me, and wished me death, just for bringing up the acronym MAGA or even bringing up any topic that is mentioned in this book.

CHAPTER 1:
PROLOGUE

"Avoid prologues: they can be annoying, especially a prologue following an introduction that comes after a foreward."[1]

Elmore Leonard

Thank goodness this prologue has been placed after the acknowledgements but preceding the introduction chapter, right?

Anyway…

In a two-party system, we might be directed to either left or right, but if we choose to vote on values and principles and truth, then there is no party of left versus right but rather foundations of right versus wrong.

This book was written with the intent not to persuade anyone to one side or the other, but to provide the reader with an accurate account of what I have discovered in my search for answers.

What is in this book is the truth of what I have discovered and it is, I think, verifiable with an accurate account of history and a true and honest conversation with those of whom we might have been inculcated to currently be viewed as dirtier and more full of crap than a septic tank pump. But I do believe that if we can clean our filters and empty our tanks of waste, then we can begin to see clearly and truly find the common thread by which our home might very well be hanging by; then, and only then, might we actually be able to stitch our family and our nation back together.

I trust that the reader will read this book with an open mind, an honest, introspective perspective, and a desire to pursue their own independent research and critical thinking in areas of life that could be vital to relationships and individual liberty.

I hope you do read this entire book and don't just skip to the main chapter, because, although I tried to keep it a short and easy read, there is a lot to unpack and digest to truly try and understand.

My hope is that the reader will not only be able to see their family, friends, neighbors, and fellow-countrymen from a potentially new perspective, one that does not involve a framed display, but that the reader will also find a new understanding and a common ground from which to build upon with them.

CHAPTER 2:
INTRODUCTION

"I do not know what I may appear to the world, but to myself I seem to have been only like a boy playing on the seashore, and diverting myself in now and then finding a smoother pebble or a prettier shell than ordinary, whilst the great ocean of truth lay all undiscovered before me."[1]

Isaac Newton

This is a short examination from my own personal research and understanding, taken by direct and indirect communication with people who clearly are, who claim to be, who identify as, and who claim they do not wear the title of it but understand MAGA and support aspects of it. It is also from my research, understanding, and perception based on actual events and actions in my life, and events, actions and political stances from those openly identifying as MAGA and those in public service who identify as, or at least support, MAGA.

You may disagree with me and my assessment. You may even claim I am a spreader of misinformation and conspiracy; and that is okay with me, because that is your free will to choose, and you have every right in a free America to voice that opinion: that is the true meaning of freedom of speech. But if you disagree, then I highly recommend you do what I did and talk directly to the source, maybe even be in the middle of the source— not with a biased attitude or an attacking mindset, but to truly and honestly search for what is true.

In fact, one area in which conspiracy is sometimes stated, is when the citizens of a nation speak of "death by a thousand cuts"; in this, liberties and freedoms are eroded slowly over a long, long period of time, and this is often done with intent. Really, we all do this to some extent in our own lives, weakening ourselves and diluting the truth of our life. Sometimes we are made aware of it and course correct and sometimes we don't and can change our destiny from life to death.

But when it comes to liberty and freedom, I have heard many different ways of defining liberty and freedom; I have even defined liberty in one of my books as "the responsible use of freedom," but I like this version that I have also heard: Freedom is not just being able to act a certain way but also being able to own your attitude, your mindset, your thinking, your beliefs—how you think and approach your circumstances. And liberty as being free to choose your way of life, your behavior, your values, your political views within a society (a nation), and being free to do so from an oppressive restriction from authority (the government). One example would be if a governing authority would impose undue and oppressive restrictions and you could no longer speak your mind (in written or verbal form) on your chosen way of life, values, belief, or political views or opinions on subject matters, then you would have lost some freedom and liberty and it probably would have occurred over time, without much notice—"death by a thousand cuts."

As I heard one person state it: there is the thesis, antithesis, and the synthesis. The thesis is, as they called it, 'what/how it is now'; the antithesis is 'what they (someone or something else) want it to be'; and the synthesis is 'the change'. In other words, there is a small, seemingly inconsequential or very minor compromise between what/how it is (the thesis) and what they want it to be (the antithesis) which then becomes the synthesis—the change, the soon to be accepted as "new normal." Then the process begins again: the "new normal" is now the thesis, there is another small compromise with the antithesis, which is now another synthesis, and, again, the soon to be accepted as "new normal." Then the process repeats, again. Soon, people do not even remember or know what the established thesis was nor do they seem to care, so long as they are conformable with the "new normal." Do these enough times (thesis compromising with antithesis producing synthesis) through enough generations and the antithesis is now fully the thesis and what was once the thesis is buried six-feet under. This is not a conspiracy, as some would say, this is a proven method. It can be a slow erosion. I think this helps some in explaining the fall of Rome—through the generations it synthesized from a flourishing economy and somewhat liberty embracing and freedom-loving Republican form of government to a Democracy where the majority ruled and individual freedoms and liberties were truly eroding without notice to so many of its citizens to an Oligarchy where freedom and liberty were outright restricted by oppressive and tyrannical Caesars (the government was now controlling the people's very lives).

You can believe that or not, it is your choice, because in a truly freedom and liberty-embracing nation, you can believe whatever you choose to believe.

In this research, and in most of my research, writings, and education, even in writing other books, posts, and podcasts, I have found that what we hear and learn from our places of education, from our political servants, from our news and media sources, from anyone, really, is not always the truth.

This should be an obvious truth, but, sometimes, we just do not see the obvious or self-evident, or we just choose to close our eyes and ears to it for one reason or another. There are times we must trust, because we cannot know everything; but even in those times it would behoove us, as much as we can, to, as the saying goes, "trust, but verify."

As I have said in other writings: What you learn from any institution or place of learning is typically in line with what those in charge of that place of education want you to know, not always what you should or need to know; it is from the foundation they have chosen to build upon, which could be biased, ignorant, unwise, manipulative, or any other form of human frailty.

Without due diligence and independent research, you only know and you can only parrot what you were told to know and what the teller wants you to parrot.

Speaking of, I remember someone who would continually back their political bias, perceived hate, and claims, by sharing various videos with random people from one social media platform, all while this person also claimed those videos were the truth, and they openly admitted that this particular social media platform was practically the only place where they get their information. That is a chosen place of learning; that is a chosen place of education.

And sometimes the information we receive from a chosen place may seem correct, it may prove our opinion or bias (which is oftentimes what people are truly after), until it is confronted with both time and challenge. "In a lawsuit, the first to speak seems right, until someone comes forward and cross-examines."[2]

In this short writing, you will read what I have discovered MAGA is and based on from what I, personally, have learned—through others, my own experiences, my involvement in politics, and independent research. As many know, "To answer before listening—that is folly and shame."[3]

If you feel otherwise, so be it; our perceptions and filters are oftentimes different, a part of what helps make each of us unique, but also what helps each of us come to different conclusions from the very same thing we are viewing and, sometimes, from the very same experience. And since many people build upon different foundations and cornerstones, the structures of our lives, the views from which our perceptions are formed from our chosen perspective, can, oftentimes, and unintentionally, be skewed.

Remember, most of what we know, we were told to know; not what we should know, not what we think we, personally, discovered to know, not what we truly believe we know, and not the truth we should know, but what one said they know and told us to know and, therefore, we now claim we truly know.

CHAPTER 3:
DO YOU TRULY...

"Picasso said, 'Art is a lie that tells the truth.' What if you just want to tell the truth and not lie about it?"[1]

Nicolas Cage

What if I said, "When they label you MAGA, wear that label proudly"? What would your immediate response be?

We've wondered, haven't we? What is it really? Could the floating heads and public servants be correct in their stereotyping? Are we truly trying to understand, or are we comfortable delegating our critical thinking to people we do not even know and accepting such a cognitive transplant?

Isn't that why you proudly claim that title? Isn't that why you wear it in secret? Isn't that why you shame, attack, ambush, lie about, discriminate against, and demolish the very Life, Liberty and pursuit of Happiness of any who would dare to wear or speak that acronym? Isn't that why we continuously jump on and fall off the wagon often in our life?

I wondered: "What is it, really? Could they be correct? Might so many have been fooled? Might we all have been beguiled?"

What I found may be a shock to you; then again, what I found might receive the response, "Yeah, I already knew that."

But first, because of all the mudslinging, defamation, misinformation, and political lies, I want to ask you some honest questions (I do hope you will answer these questions for yourself, and I hope you do answer them honestly):

- Do you like your freedom?

- Do you like your liberty?

- Do you like the right to Life, Liberty, and the pursuit of [your] Happiness?

- Do you like your country (for me that would be the United States of America)?

- Do you, in America, consider yourself more of a Constitutionalist—someone who supports the Constitution and our founding ideals as they were established and truly are above any one political party or ideology of "ism"?

I think most of us would answer those questions with a resounding, "YES!"

I also think most of us would proudly say that we have "love for or devotion to [our] country,"[2] therefore, we would consider ourselves patriots.

I have wondered, sometimes, how many of us would actually say we have "love [for our] country; the passion which aims to serve [our] country, either in defending it from invasion, or protecting its rights and maintaining its laws and institutions in vigor and purity"?[3] That is: we boldly defend the laws, institutions, ideals, values, and Constitution as it was written and intended—its purity—and not want to or support the violation of, the weakening of, or the polluting of that founding purity; therefore, we would consider ourselves patriots.

Again, if I asked, "Do you love your freedom, right to Life, Liberty, and the pursuit of [your] Happiness? Do you consider yourself more of a Constitutionalist, someone who understood self-evident, someone who believed in unalienable rights," and added, "would you consider yourself an American patriot?" I think most of us would still answer with a resounding, "YES!" Because most of us do love our country; we just have different opinions and follow different ideas of what makes, or would make, this a country that we love.

I think most of us, if we were to answer based on our own experience, reason, and logic, and if we truly were to give an honest answer, would clearly say that it is great when we follow the wisdom of our founders and God (whether or not you believe in Him is irrelevant here, because there are "laws of nature" that God put in place, and when you follow them, you get certain results, whether you are a believer or not). But I think most of us would agree that it is great when our country is energy independent, flourishing economically, embracing the freedom to worship, helping its very neighbors and family (citizens), and seeing record job growth and fewer and fewer people unemployed or on government assistance, just to name a few things. This is, I think, a common ground that most of us can agree on and begin to build upon.

"By their fruit you will recognize them. Do people pick grapes from thornbushes, or figs from thistles?"[4]

I do think that most of us would love to see our country, the great United States of America, be the land of innovation, productivity, hope, and the beacon of freedom and prosperity that so many people in the world seek. But that cannot happen if we are not both vigilant and planting good seeds, seeds that will produce a plentiful harvest, seeds that will spread to bring Life, Liberty, and the pursuit of Happiness to everyone living in the land.

We all have a private life—what are you

planting in private? Will it, whatever you are choosing to plant, produce good fruit?

Those in high positions of authority don't just plant a seed, they sow seeds into a large crop, into a plantation, and the harvest will be evident to all living under their authority. The question then is: do we celebrate the harvest or do we cut it down and plow and cultivate the land with seeds known for their nutrient and plentiful harvest?

Unfortunately, in a free land, you have intercropping, which is the cultivation of two or more crops simultaneously on the same field. Then again, you cannot have true freedom and individual liberty if you do not also allow such differing crops on the same land, even when they will sometimes cause struggles and clash.

Do you like your freedom and liberties?

By their continued works, you will know their true heart.

Do you truly understand what freedom means? What liberty means? The truth of tolerance? The First Amendment: "Congress shall make no law...abridging (that is, shortening or depriving anyone of) the freedom of speech...and to petition (which is, a formal written request—even online) the Government for a redress (*or remedy, correction*) of grievances (the person's expression: grief, suffering, disapproval, distress)."[5]

Sometimes we can control our speech; we can plan and prepare pre-written teachings or speeches, which are carefully planned to elicit a certain emotion or response; and with that, we can deceive people and attempt to distract them from our very actions.

Do we make our judgment based on the fruit, the words, or our emotional state?

Thomas Jefferson said, "A wise and frugal government, which shall restrain men from injuring one another, shall leave them otherwise free to regulate their own pursuits of industry and improvement, and shall not take from the mouth of labor the bread it has earned."[6]

"But the things that come out of a person's mouth come from the heart..."[7]

Do you truly judge by the fruit? The words? Or by emotion?

"...do not believe every spirit, but test the spirits..."[8]

Do not believe every person, but test them by their fruit.

Do they produce good crops? Do they produce crops of hope, of freedom, of liberty, of life, of help, of inspiration, of plenty, of growth? Or do they produce crops of fear, of dependence, of regulations, of death, of stress, of disincentive, of scarcity, or retard growth?

It reminds me of that old proverb, that great and wise saying: "Trust, but verify."

For those like me who believe in God, we ask, do they line up with God's Word?

The answer is: not always. Then again, there is no one, anymore, who will line up one hundred percent with God's word or with what is truly good and just, because we are all human; and we each have our faults and failings. "…for all have sinned and fallen short…"[9] With that, there can never be a nation on this earth, at least for now, that will line up one hundred percent with biblical teachings, with what is just and right and good, with what we might desire; that will offer full and complete liberty and freedom without some small amount of constraint; that will truly always be for the people; that will have a government and servants full of love and compassion and free from selfish desires or greed. However, there is one nation, and only one nation, that has come closer than any other in history. It was an experiment, something that was never thought of or done before, but it worked and it worked well. And this, I think, is worth defending and fighting to keep. But that is just my opinion and my belief from my research, learning, and understanding.

You may think differently, and that is okay; but if you do, then there are other places whose values and belief systems of how governments should be implemented and managed, as well as what and how the people living under such a government should think and act, which will more closely line up with your belief and values and understanding; and I'm sure each of these places would welcome you with open arms, embracing all immigrants... maybe. We would just need to take some time to observe where oppressed people are fleeing to.

We all have our differing experiences, perceptions, and various levels of education, knowledge and understanding. Interestingly, we can see, feel, experience and be affected by the same situation and, yet, we can leave it with two completely different perspectives: one good and full of hope and growth, and one bad and full of fear and regress.

As the saying goes, two people can look at the exact same thing and see something totally different.

CHAPTER 4:
I WONDER... A BACKSTORY

"Wisdom begins in wonder."[1]

Socrates

There has been so much said and so much ignored and so much misassumption (yes, this is actually a word. I looked it up) that, it would feel like, we are left with only three options: One, believe everything we are being told, without question; Two, disbelieve everything we are being told, without question—one and two would require of us to disregard our own thinking and be slothful in our research—or Three, do independent research and draw conclusions from independent thinking.

So, I began to research and use critical thinking in my search for answers.

I pondered: What if my own previous judgments were construed from unfounded, blind trust? What if my opinion was not truly mine but one implanted by repetition?

I wondered: What if they are right? Then again, what if they are wrong?

I asked: What is MAGA?

What if I said, "When they label you MAGA, wear that label proudly"? What would your immediate response be?

According to you: does just saying that phrase make me "extreme," a "terrorist," a "white supremacist," a "threat to democracy," a "fascist," a "xenophobic," a "sexist," "homophobic," "deplorable," an "enemy of the state," a "domestic enemy," "racist," "intolerant," a "murderer," a part of a "death cult," a "white nationalist," a "Nazi," a "conspiracy theorist," a "religious zealot," etc.?

These are just a few of the terms I have heard and read (even directed toward me just for asking questions) that are used to describe anyone who is MAGA, who we think might be MAGA, or who would even dare to wear or say the word MAGA or the phrase I said... even though I added the disclaimer "What if I said..."

Do we make our judgment based on the fruit, the words, or our emotional state?

I wondered if maybe, just maybe, what the political left, the current office holder of President, Joe Biden, and his administration, some educators, a plethora of Hollywood and other elites, the "mostly peaceful" groups of BLM and Antifa, and a lot of the news media, were correct in their labeling of those who support, vote in line with and want to make America great again?

I wondered if maybe they are right.

We hear it a lot: it is parroted, like clockwork, almost like a scripted play, the same lines and phrases; sometimes, almost exactly word-for-word.

If they are right, then that means our democracy is at stake, our founding (the parts we wish to accept) is in jeopardy, and our freedoms and liberties—as granted by the government, because if not from God, then from man—are being misapplied.

If they are wrong, then that means our Constitutional Republic is at stake, our founding (the whole) is in jeopardy, and our freedoms and liberties—as granted by God, not man—are being abused.

As I say in other writings: God-given is null and void if God there not be.

That is why I decided to do some research, and I actually took the time to talk with people—not harassed or vilified or assassinated their character, but talked.

I know what I believe; I know what I have seen, witnessed, lived, and experienced; I know what I have been educated with and by; I know what I have found from my own independent research and from critical thinking; and I know who I am. There is no confusion there.

What I have found, and what should be completely obvious, is that there is so much misinformation out there being spread by fallacious (*deceiving/misleading*) arguments, erroneous (*errored/wrong/incorrect*) assumptions, perfidious (*faithless/disloyal*) talking heads, and two-faced (*insincere/deceitful*) political servants.

Hey, there is another common ground for the citizens, all people, regardless of political affiliation, in this scorching political climate—maybe that is the climate change we should focus on.

(It's okay. You can laugh at my dumb jokes, even in a serious book.)

Anyway, I have found that if you really want to know something, then the best way to find out is to talk to those involved—go to the source...if you can. You will not always get the truth from people, but you can get better information and be closer to the truth by taking this step.

This reminds me of a time, many, many years ago, when there were political groups holding rallies and one was in my area. Well, after the rally, I noticed someone I knew posted on social media what they had learned from a media source about how the people at the rally were racist, hateful, and trashed the place they were at. I knew this was a lie because I had decided to see what these rallies were all about and how the people actually acted at one of them, and so I attended this particular rally of which this person was spreading misinformation about. I was even there after everyone left and the place was clean.

It is still amazing to me, though, how we can (and we all do it sometimes) speak of wanting to know the truth, proclaim that we know the truth, and, yet, still not once care to open The Book, speak to those with direct or similar experience, do any type of independent research, even try to go to the source, listen to another perspective, or even acknowledge the truth when we do find it. We, sometimes, just close our eyes, plug our ears, shout the parroted phrases, and then receive our cracker.

This reminds me of when I worked in education. I was at a place of higher learning and, where I was working, we got to meet so many foreign students. It was great. We had the privilege to listen to and learn from those who grew up in and experienced different cultures, governments, and political climates. In all my time there and with all the foreign students we talked with—students from around the world: students whose parents fled certain socialist and communist countries or who they, themselves, fled as well, with their parents—well, not one of them, that I can recall, spoke well of their government. They loved their country, but we were told that because of socialism and communism, which permeated their government and country, they were not free; they did not have near the freedoms or liberties we have in America, and there was much oppression, suppression, and cancelling of the people and opposition: suppression of thought, speech, and anything that went against the governmental powers in charge; and there were limits on the many things we take for granted here in America: food, electricity, income, time, etc.

I also remember many instructors trying to inform those same students that they were completely wrong. I remember one in particular who told the student that their parents were liars, they should not trust their parents when they speak about socialism, and that they (the student and their parents) do not know what true socialism is, because true socialism, according to the instructor, is great and the best thing for society.

What are you planting in private? Will it produce good fruit?

It is interesting to me how we can talk directly with people involved in something or who have lived under something and then immediately dismiss them, their perception, their knowledge, their understanding, their experience, their very life itself, if it is in direct contrast to our own selfish desire or political opinion (I guess, in these cases, I should say political bias).

As I have said many times in other writings, we all build our lives from a foundation. Some foundations are firm and absolute, some are weak and unstable and ever-changing. And, sometimes, a political party can become someone's god, the very foundation upon which they build their values, standards, morals, and life upon.

Anyway, in my research, I have talked with those, both in person and online, who directly identify as MAGA. I have read their posts, talked directly with many of them, and looked at what they claim to stand for in their lives and politically (what they would and are voting for on the ballots, and what their values are and what their stances are on current issues), and I have talked to and read stuff from people who do not, openly at least, claim to identify as MAGA for one reason or another (more often, I think, it is because of fear for life or livelihood), but who willingly and publicly gave their opinions on what they believe MAGA is. I have also talked with and read from people who are clearly not MAGA. And this is the information I have concluded.

If you want to know better, then go directly to the source...if you can.

Keep this in mind: these are our friends, neighbors, family, strangers, fellow Americans; many people you might know—a father or mother, brother or sister, your child; and it may very well be you reading this book.

Like I said before, this is what I have concluded based on my research and findings and understanding. You might come to a very different perspective based on your perception of life and those of whom you share life with; and that is expected, because we do not all view life through the same lens or filter, nor do we all choose to seek the truth, and that is what helps make each of us unique, and it is what free will, freedom, and liberty are all about.

And if I am honest with you, my values and beliefs and standards line more greatly with what I have found here than what I have found from other philosophies and political ideas. And if you are honest, too, then I believe you might very well find common ground from which to build upon with your family, friends, neighbors, and fellow citizens.

CHAPTER 5:
WHAT IS MAGA?

"It will be found an unjust and unwise jealousy to deprive a man of his natural liberty upon the supposition he may abuse it."[1]

George Washington

Here is what I have discovered in my search for answers.

1

WHAT IS MAGA

MAGA is not the name of a person, neither is it sole-support for any person or political party.

It is a philosophy, a movement, an idea that says, "I love my country. I put my country first. I agree with the Founding Fathers, our founding documents and ideals and values, individual liberty, accountability, security, Constitutional law and God-given rights, and I want to see my country prosper."

It does not declare that you or I ignore any of our country's past, nor does it purposefully rewrite the past to fit in line with a modern idea of enlightenment that we are the most moral, ethical, educated, talented, loving, knowing, and god-like people, therefore we can ignore our current but ever-changing and fluctuating chosen set of values, ethics, and morals, or all of history; and, therefore, we can and must judge all of history by our current self-proposed self-righteousness—censoring what we deem as subversive, rewriting that which does not fit out current chosen agenda, tearing down that which we choose to find offensive, and discarding that which "dirties" our current chosen norms and self-enlightenment.

It understands the difference between its country and its government; and it proudly supports, defends, celebrates, and honors its country.

It understands the desire for reeducation by its home's enemy, "If you can cut the people off from their history, then they can be easily persuaded."[2] — Karl Marx.

MAGA says, "I understand we are not what we once were—we have allowed our values, morals, founding ideals, to be warped by outside and failed philosophies and an ever-growing, opposite of our founding, overreaching governmental body—but we can become that shining city, that beacon of light and hope, set on a hill again; we can be the land of freedom and liberty with rights granted by God ("endowed by our Creator," "the laws of nature and natures God"); we can be the land of hope for those seeking refuge from tyranny, censorship, figurative and literal cancelation for daring to think or speak of God or any opinion opposite of their government or those serving in governmental roles of authority; we can be a land of refuge from persecution, religious execution and muzzling, and a land where all people can work hard, take risk and provide better lives for themselves and their family. We can be that land, again, that we were founded to be: self-governed; a limited and small government; God-inspired; a land of opportunity; a land of freedom and liberty; a land (government) of the people, by the people, for the people; a land acknowledging the intrinsic value of life; a land of personal responsibility and accountability; and a land of greatness.

2

MAGA MEANS WE ARE NOT PERFECT, BUT WE CAN RETURN TO THE GREATNESS THAT MADE AMERICA:

The Constitution, Declaration; a land of individual liberty.

MAGA says, "We have fought long and costly battles to ensure America's founding ideals that every person's God-given unalienable rights to Life, Liberty and the pursuit of Happiness are secured and not infringed, and we have come a long way to right the wrongs of the past and of the world, to become a nation set apart from the oppressive government systems in place in the world, and to grow in understanding, freedom of thought and speech, and where 'all men are created equal.'"

MAGA understands equal does not mean equal in outcome but equal in freedom to Life, Liberty and the pursuit of Happiness to reach a desired and prosperous outcome—the outcomes will be different.

3

FREEDOM OF RELIGION

MAGA says, "Let each worship freely, in public and private, and attend their place of worship. And if I don't agree, so be it; it is everyone's right."

MAGA says that each person has the right and freedom to worship, and that a government does not have the power to override the God-given rights of people to attend their chosen place of worship.

Although it is not tied to one religion, it understands the snare of its home's enemy: "The Christian religion and National Socialist doctrines are not compatible."[3] — Martin

Bormann (head of the Nazi Part Chancellery)

It holds to the Constitution: "Congress [the government: federal, state, and local] shall make no law respecting the establishment of religion, or prohibiting the free exercise thereof [of religion]."[4]

It remembers its home's history when one of the first acts of the first Continental Congress was to hold a prayer meeting, which lasted nearly two hours and involved the reading of Psalm 35 from the Holy Bible.

4

FREEDOM FROM TYRANNY

MAGA says, "We are a free people. Our ancestors fled from and fought against tyranny and authoritarian governments to provide people with a land of Liberty."

It says that a nation and its people should not be subservient to an abject or overreaching government or governmental power; that the people of a nation should not be forced under tyranny to abandon their God or to attend one church or to believe in one religion or denomination—as was most of the world and is part of the world (my personal belief: although to claim one is an athiest is to make the claim that one knows all, which is illogical and irrational, atheism is a religion, as can be a political party)— that God be center and present (allowed) in public, private, government and education as was the written and documented intention of our founding and Founding Fathers, whether the individual believes in God or not; that those in public office serve the people and not force the people to serve them.

5

LOVE AND PROTECT, PUT YOUR HOME AND FAMILY FIRST

MAGA says, "I want to make America, the land that I choose to live in and the land that I love, great again."

It understands that, just like your personal family and home, you cannot make it great without putting it first and your family—the legal citizens—first.

It understands that to protect your family, you build security (walls, fences, gates, borders) to keep unwanted people and bad things out, and that you vet (are selective about) the people who you let into your home and be a part of your family—not because you are prejudiced or hateful toward anyone, but because you understand that space and resources will be limited, that the cost in all areas would be greater, as would the undue burden on your family, and because you love your family and want to protect them and the best for them.

It welcomes those who enter their home legally, who want the best for their new home (America), and who assimilate, as they are supposed to, to the rules and laws of their new home.

MAGA understands that without borders, a nation is not a nation; and without clear borders and the protection and enforcement of those borders, there is little sovereignty or distinction between citizen and alien. That each of us, MAGA and non-MAGA, put walls and fences and doors with locks around our own homes and family, and that this nation is our home and the legal citizens are our family.

6

LAW OF THE LAND

MAGA says, "There is a law of the land, The Constitution of the United States of America, that must be held dear and protected and enforced."

It understands that the laws and rules of your home apply to all who step foot inside, and that the benefits and privileges graciously granted to and set forth for your family are not to be stolen, demanded of, or arbitrarily given to all who would climb your fence, bust your walls down, break your locks, disrespect and disregard your family and cross your home's border uninvited, illegally, violating your very rules and laws and putting your family in danger and at risk, and taking without consent from your family what was and is legally and justly theirs.

It understands compassion, but it also understands that to embrace a lawbreaker at the expense of and to cause greater suffering to your family is not to love your family.

MAGA says that "This land—America— is my home, those legal citizens, even though we might disagree and argue, are my family, and that if I love my home and family, I must put them first and protect their lives and their God-given rights, even if I vehemently disagree. And that if I allow another to enter my home, then as a new member of my family, they must assimilate to my home's laws and support the very home they have chosen to reside in."

7

FREEDOM OF SPEECH

MAGA says, "I may very well not agree with or even like what you say, and although we might argue, I understand you have the very same freedoms and rights to speech that I do; therefore, I will not demand that you be canceled, fired, muzzled, just because I don't want to hear or read it or because I claim I am offended by what you said or posted."

It does not always agree with another's opinion, but it accepts that your opinions, perceptions, beliefs, and personal values might very well be different or even opposite of them, but you have the same right to voice and post and write and speak those opinions; and it will not silence, cancel, or shut down your voice just because you do not agree or speak what it wants to hear or what it wants you to say: MAGA understands what freedom of speech is.

8

INCLUSIVE

MAGA says, "You can be any race, color, ethnicity, gender, even someone not born in America, and be welcomed, so long as you are legally and lawfully here and love America, its founding documents, and wish to see it put first and be great."

It acknowledges that you can be labeled a Democrat and be MAGA; you can be labeled a Republican and be MAGA; you can be labeled an Independent, Libertarian, or non-political, and still be MAGA. It also acknowledges that you can be labeled a Democrat or Republican or any of the others and be an enemy of its home and its family.

MAGA is not white supremacy; it is not homophobic; it is not anti-immigrant; it is not anti-feminine; it is not anti-government; it is not anti-Constitution; it is not anti-

American; it be no respecter of gender or color or ethnicity. It welcomes all colors and races; it welcomes male and female; it welcomes all people who love their home, their family, the truth of its ideals, values and founding, who have the desire to see their home and family thrive and be independent, and who follow its founding documents.

9
POLITICAL UNDERSTANDING

MAGA says, "I have seen, read, and learned about history; I have not closed my eyes to it or rewritten it to embellish it and beguile my family to the "isms" of perpetual historical tragedy."

MAGA understands that America was founded as a Republic—it was and is supposed to be a Constitutional Republic, not a Democracy.

It understands what James Madison

stated: "...democracies have ever been spectacles of turbulence and contention; have ever been found incompatible with personal security or the rights of property; and have in general been as short in their lives as they have been violent in their deaths."[5]

It understands the subtle persuasion of its home's enemy: "Democracy is the road to socialism."[6] — Karl Marx

It understands that the philosophies and governments of Socialism, Marxism, and Communism are one, and that they are in direct opposition to America's Constitution and founding documents; and they are antithetical to Life, Liberty and the pursuit of Happiness, to America's founding ideals, to God, to freedom and liberty, and to America itself.

It understands the goal of its home's enemy: "The goal of socialism is communism."[7] —Vladimir Ilyich Lenin

MAGA is not fascist. It understands that fascism calls for a strong, often dictatorial, central government that controls all industry and commerce. It understands that fascists have no tolerance for those who do not validate, accept, and participate in their beliefs or lifestyle or opinions; that fascists have no desire for discussion and no tolerance for freedom of expression or opposing views. It understands that fascists also emphasize a specific race or group over the individual and individual rights; and they use force and fear and mandates to suppress all opposition and criticism.

It understands the truth in the phrase "to control the body, you must first control the mind." It understands the steps of the "isms" which are the enemy of its home: nationalize education, control the flow of information, and criminalize dissension.

It understands that we are sovereign states who created a small and limited government, not the other way around.

It understands that a government too large and too powerful (the opposite of what our Founding Fathers intended) can easily be corrupted by one party or one group or the "isms" contrary to its foundation. It knows, from history, that such a government could become politically motivated, tyrannical, and abuse its own agencies and limited power.

It agrees with Thomas Jefferson and our Founding Fathers about a small and limited government: "Our legislators are not sufficiently apprized of the rightful limits of their power; that their true office is to declare and enforce only our natural rights and duties, and to take none of them from us."[8]

10

CHARITY

MAGA says, "I love my home and my family. I put them first. If they are in need, I would prefer my resources go to my family first to help them get back on their feet by giving them a hand up, not a handout."

MAGA does not ignore, forget, look down upon, or wish the death of those less fortunate—MAGA is pro-life. It understands and comprehends, whether or not it directly agrees with a certain religion, that, although the government's intentions may be well in the beginning, the Churches provide the most help to the poor, widowed, and desolate than any government program ever could or has; and the private sector is the next in line. And it understands that America has been the most blessed and generous country, offering its finances, resources, ideas, and even its citizens' very lives, to those in distress around the world.

11
CANCEL CULTURE & TYRANNY

MAGA says, "I will defend your God-given unalienable rights because I know they are not granted by man or by the government;

they are natural, God-given, unalienable rights that our Constitution (which does not grant you those rights) clearly protects by limiting the government's power to tyrannically infringe on your very rights."

MAGA does not force its opposition to cancellation; it does not force submission through suppression, oppression, aggression, tyranny, big-government overreach, mandates of fear for life, livelihood, health, social ability and status, education, service to country, or freedom to worship.

It understands that, even if it disagrees or has trepidation with a God-given unalienable right, it will not force you to relinquish your very right.

It understands the worry of its home's enemy: "Ideas are more powerful than guns. We would not let our enemies have guns, why should we let them have ideas."[9] — Joseph Stalin.

12

GOVERNMENT & HANDOUTS

MAGA says, "Government does not create; it is established to help protect."

It understands the common heard saying that "the essence of freedom is the proper limitation of government."

It has heard and read what Thomas Jefferson, when writing what is known as "Jefferson's Draft," was trying to explain, "that the several states composing the US. of America are not united on the principle of unlimited submission to their general government...reserving, each state to itself, the residuary mass of right to their own self-government; and that whensoever the General government assumes undelegated powers, it's acts are unauthoritative, void, and of no force." And, "the government created... was not made the exclusive or final judge of the extent of the powers delegated to itself; since that would have made it's discretion, and not the constitution the measure of it's powers..."[10]

It understands that a government only has what it takes, justly and unjustly, from the people; that a government can only give what was someone else's first. That the government is to govern foreign affairs and protect the unalienable God-given rights of the citizens. That, as Thomas Jefferson put it, "The policy of American government is to leave its citizens free, neither restraining them nor aiding them in their pursuits."[11]

13

TOLERANCE

MAGA says, "I don't have to like your foundation, nor do I have to participate in or even acknowledge the support of your foundation or lifestyle to still love you or tolerate you. I know you are not just what you do or how you choose to live."

It understands that tolerance is not participation in or acceptance of a lifestyle, philosophy, belief, or a violation of personal values to appease the feelings or false belief of inadequacy in another, but that tolerance is knowing that the person is more than and not just the lifestyle they choose or their current emotional state.

14

LIFE

MAGA says, "Life is precious. We should not grow cold-hearted and terminate a life just because we feel burdened by that life or because we did not have that life scheduled on our calendar."

It understands that life is intrinsic (it holds value all its own) and not measured by the perceived quality of its accomplishments or lack thereof, lifestyle choice, or potential burden; and that you can live your life and I can live mine and we can still love and tolerate each other even if we do not agree; but it also understands that sometimes you must fight to protect your home and family.

It also understands that there are consequences for the choices made in life, and that life, although intrinsically valuable, can be rendered short based on the personal choices of the person living that life.

15

CHILDREN, THE NEXT GENERATION

MAGA says, "Child-rearing, although difficult sometimes, is a duty of the parent (if there is no parent, then the legal guardian). Children are a blessing; and children, although being very naïve and trusting, which also helps make children very impressionable to the molding of outside forces, are justly and rightfully the responsibility of the parent to raise and, therefore, should not be subjected to the propagandizing of political, social, sexual or emotional confusion in the education system."

MAGA wants to protect children and the parental rights of those children. It is not wanting or allowing total government or state control of its children, or even your children without your consent. It is knowing that you cannot protect children if you are also ending their lives. It understands that protecting children and parental rights is not the blind or willful support of state and government control from "domestic terrorists" (I.E., parents) over their own children, nor is it protecting children and parental rights to allow government control of sexual, emotional, mental and physical manipulation and mutilation of children, especially without parental knowledge.

It understands that children are impressionable. They are and always have been a primary target of governmental entities and political philosophies seeking control and power.

It knows the target of its home's enemy: "Give me just one generation of youth, and I'll transform the whole world."[12] — Vladimir Ilyich Lenin

MAGA understands that public education is not about feelings or pronouns or a political ideology of social scores or shaming for being born in a certain skin color, but about the real-world skills and understanding of reading, writing, math, science, history, and technology. It understands that a place of education is a place of diverse thought, of critical thinking, of helping the student in the solidifying of the student's chosen moral character. It is a place to be challenged, and it is a place to do the challenging. It is a place for further growth. It is not a place of censoring ideas, opinions, questions, or political thinking that differs from the person doing the educating or what the education centers' governing authority likes or supports.

It knows the playbook of its home's enemy: "Give me four years to teach the children and the seed I have sown will never be uprooted."[13] — Vladimir Ilyich Lenin

It understands that you are not born an oppressor or oppressed just because of the color of your skin, but that you become one or the other by the actions you choose—the character you allow to be instilled in your life, and the character you (or, if you insist, your political, governmental system) instills in your children.

It knows that Noah Webster was correct when he said, "The education of youth should be watched with the most scrupulous attention. [I]t is much easier to introduce and establish an effectual system ... than to correct by penal statutes the ill effects of a bad system. ... The education of youth ... lays the foundations on which both law and gospel rest for success."[14]

16

FAMILY

It understands that the nuclear family is important for the development of proper and good morals and values in the home and society, and that the hierarchy of the nuclear family is good; it is not, as some would claim, a unit of consumption that teaches subservience or hordes wealth, passing it to their children in order to reproduce class inequality.

It has seen the tactics of its home's enemy: "Destroy the family, you destroy the country."[15]

It understands that "a good person leaves an inheritance for their children's children."[16]

17

PUBLIC SERVICE

MAGA says, "Public service is about serving the public, serving your home, taking the oath to defend your home and family, and to abide by the rule of law and the law of the land—our Constitution."

MAGA understands that the government and those in government services work for the people, not the other way around. It understands that laws and benefits paid for by the legal citizens and set forth for the legal citizens, for the nation, for your home and family, cannot and should not be taken and freely given to the world, to those who break into our home, lest our home's laws and rules and benefits be that of the word's, in which case there is no home— no America—but America is the world and we, therefore, have an obligation to and we must enforce our ways upon the entire world.

18
CONCLUSIONS

MAGA is for the return of America's founding—our ideals, our Constitution, our God-given unalienable rights, our freedom of speech and thought, our understanding and comprehension that, yes, we are to help each other (our family) as best as we can, but each is responsible for their own actions, good or bad; that these truths once again be self-evident; that government must be what it was intended and established to be: small, for foreign affairs, and to protect the God-given unalienable rights and life of its lawful citizens; and that we put our home and our family first again.

And, MAGA is the hope that America can be and will remain the last best hope, that shining beacon upon a hill, that land of freedom, and the most innovative and prosperous nation in history—all thanks to God, the willingness and bravery of our Founding Fathers to sacrifice everything to fight tyranny and dictators, our God-given unalienable rights, and the greatest governmental document in history: The Constitution of the United States of America.

It has felt the implementation of its home's enemy: (Although it has been stated that this was just an accurate paraphrase of what Lenin said, it still holds true to that philosophical mindset of 'ism,') "The way to crush the bourgeoisie is to grind them between the millstones of taxation and inflation."[17]

I would like to end with this interview with Xi Van Fleet, a survivor of socialism. She fled the socialist regime of China for the freedom and liberty of America; that same freedom and liberty that many who are living under socialism and communism seek, of which many in America, who are blessed to be born in, spit upon.

"I just want to say it's so ironic. 36 years ago, I run away from socialism when

I left China to come to this great country for freedom. Today, so many Americans [are] abandoning freedom and arriving into socialism. They have no idea what socialism is about. I lived under Mao's socialism. When the government controls everything and makes all the decisions big and small and decide how much grain, meat [and] cooking oil I could have. What I should learn in school, where I should live, and what job I should have and how I should think. In the socialist society I lived under, there was no choices. There is no freedom. And that's what people do not know. Socialism becomes such a diluted word and it's intentional. I can tell you, China is a socialist country. Cuba is a socialist country and so is North Korea. They are a socialist country run by communist parties. And what's the difference? What's the difference between socialism and communism? Not much. Socialism is the initial stage of communism, according to Karl Marx."[18]

There could be more to MAGA that

was not discussed here, but that is for your own independent research.

As for my search for answers, this is what I have discovered:

MAGA is the opposite of tyranny, of anarchy, of self-abasement, of oppression, of Socialism, of Marxism, and of Communism.

MAGA is for freedom and Life, Liberty, and the pursuit of Happiness.

MAGA embraces all who wish to see their home remain free, the Constitution be upheld and enforced once again, America to remain that beacon of hope, their home to be independent and sovereign and prosperous, their family to retain their God-given unalienable rights, and America to be great again.

That is why I have concluded:
When they label you MAGA, wear that label proudly.

BIBLIOGRAPHY

ACKNOWLEDGMENTS:

1. "William Arthur Ward Quotes." BrainyQuote. com. BrainyMedia Inc, 2022. 14 September 2022. https://www.brainyquote.com/quotes/ william_arthur_ward_105497

CHAPTER 1: PROLOGUE

1. "Elmore Leonard." AZQuotes.com. Wind and Fly LTD, 2022. 17 September 2022. https://www.azquotes.com/quote/730311

CHAPTER 2: INTRODUCTION

1. "Isaac Newton Quotes." BrainyQuote.com. BrainyMedia Inc, 2022. 4 September 2022. https://www.brainyquote.com/quotes/ isaac_newton_387031
2. The Holy Bible, New International Version. Grand Rapids: Zondervan House, 1984.

Print.

    a. Proverbs 18:17

3. The Holy Bible, New International Version. Grand Rapids: Zondervan House, 1984. Print.

    a. Proverbs 18:13

CHAPTER 3: DO YOU TRULY...

1. "Nicolas Cage Quotes." BrainyQuote.com. BrainyMedia Inc, 2022. 5 September 2022. https://www.brainyquote.com/quotes/nicolas_cage_583650

2. "Patriotism Definition & Meaning." Merriam-Webster, Merriam-Webster, https://www.merriam-webster.com/dictionary/patriotism.

3. Countryman, Jack and Dr. Richard G. Lee. God's Promises for the American Patriot. Nashville, Tennessee, Thomas Nelson, 2011.

4. The Holy Bible, New International Version. Grand Rapids: Zondervan House, 1984. Print.

    a. Matthew 7:16

5. The Constitution of the United States with

Index, and the Declaration of Independence. second ed., National Center for Constitutional Studies, 2019.

6. "Thomas Jefferson Quotes." BrainyQuote. com. BrainyMedia Inc, 2022. 4 September 2022. https://www.brainyquote.com/quotes/ thomas_jefferson_564175

7. The Holy Bible, New International Version. Grand Rapids: Zondervan House, 1984. Print.

   a. Matthew 15:18

8. The Holy Bible, New International Version. Grand Rapids: Zondervan House, 1984. Print.

   a. 1 John 4:1

9. The Holy Bible, New International Version. Grand Rapids: Zondervan House, 1984. Print.

   a. Romans 3:23

CHAPTER 4: I WONDER… A BACKSTORY

1. "Socrates Quotes." BrainyQuote.com. BrainyMedia Inc, 2022. 5 September 2022.

https://www.brainyquote.com/quotes/socrates_101211

CHATPER 5: WHAT IS MAGA?

1. "George Washington Quotes." BrainyQuote. com. BrainyMedia Inc, 2022. 5 September 2022. https://www.brainyquote.com/quotes/george_washington_118082
2. "Karl Marx." AZQuotes.com. Wind and Fly LTD, 2022. 06 September 2022. https://www.azquotes.com/quote/189353
3. "Martin Bormann." AZQuotes.com. Wind and Fly LTD, 2022. 14 September 2022. https://www.azquotes.com/quote/699082
4. The Constitution of the United States with Index, and the Declaration of Independence. second ed., National Center for Constitutional Studies, 2019.
5. "Federalist Papers No. 10 (1787)." Bill of Rights Institute, https://billofrightsinstitute.org/primary-sources/federalist-no-10.
6. "Karl Marx." AZQuotes.com. Wind and Fly LTD, 2022. 06 September 2022. https://www.azquotes.com/quote/189353

7. "Vladimir Lenin Quotes." BrainyQuote.com. BrainyMedia Inc, 2022. 6 September 2022. https://www.brainyquote.com/quotes/vladimir_lenin_136421

8. "Thomas Jefferson." AZQuotes.com. Wind and Fly LTD, 2022. 14 September 2022. https://www.azquotes.com/quote/572186

9. "Joseph Stalin." AZQuotes.com. Wind and Fly LTD, 2022. 14 September 2022. https://www.azquotes.com/quote/280670

10. "I. Jefferson's Draft, [before 4 October 1798]," Founders Online, National Archives, https://founders.archives.gov/documents/Jefferson/01-30-02-0370-0002. [Original source: The Papers of Thomas Jefferson, vol. 30, 1 January 1798–31 January 1799, ed. Barbara B. Oberg. Princeton: Princeton University Press, 2003, pp. 536–543.]

11. Mr. Liberty. "Founding Fathers on Freedom, Liberty and American Exceptionalism." In Search of Liberty, 26 Jan. 2018, https://www.insearchofliberty.com/founding-fathers-on-freedom-liberty-and-american-exceptionalism/.

12. "Vladimir Lenin." AZQuotes.com Wind and

Fly LTD, 2022. 06 September 2022. https://www.azquotes.com/quote/370514

13. "Vladimir Lenin Quotes." BrainyQuote.com. BrainyMedia Inc, 2022. 6 September 2022. https://www.brainyquote.com/quotes/vladimir_lenin_153238

14. "Noah Webster." AZQuotes.com. Wind and Fly LTD, 2022. 06 September 2022. https://www.azquotes.com/quote/819154

15. "Vladimir Lenin Quotes." BrainyQuote.com. BrainyMedia Inc, 2022. 6 September 2022. https://www.brainyquote.com/quotes/vladimir_lenin_125951

16. The Holy Bible, New International Version. Grand Rapids: Zondervan House, 1984. Print.

    a. Proverbs 13:22

17. "Vladimir Lenin Quotes." BrainyQuote.com. BrainyMedia Inc, 2022. 6 September 2022. https://www.brainyquote.com/quotes/vladimir_lenin_125951

18. "Communist China Survivor Issues Warning to Americans: Socialism Is Only the First Stage." MSN, https://www.msn.com/en-us/news/world/communist-china-

survivor-issues-warning-to-americans-socialism-is-only-the-first-stage/ar-AA11aoow?ocid=U452DHP&li=BBnb7Kz.

ABOUT THE AUTHOR

Josh C. Jones is a media contractor, writer and podcaster, and he has experience in filmmaking, entertainment, politics, education, and public speaking. He is also published by two different publishing companies.

He is the author of *Destiny: Life or Death, Choose Your Destiny*, where he explains the five traits that each of us have by which we can control our destiny and live a life of good character. He is also the author of *ENTREPRENEUR: Road Map For Success*, where he discusses the five characteristics he has found, during his time so far as an entrepreneur, in successful and respected people; characteristics we can all choose to incorporate into our lives to better reach our success and build a life of good character.

He has a bachelor's degree in media from Oral Roberts University, graduating Cum Laude.

Josh has four more books written just waiting in the queue to be published.

Josh C. Jones has a passion to bring the Truth, common sense, hope, understanding, insight and entertainment to people through his writings and creativity. One of his goals is to change the perspective for a better understanding.

You can hear more from Josh on his audio podcast *From My Standpoint.*

ALSO, BY JOSH C. JONES

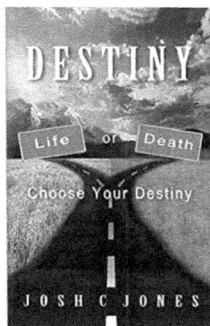

Destiny: Life or Death, Choose Your Destiny

This book is a powerful revelation on the power that we have over our own lives.

What if someone told you that you are destined for more?

What if someone told you that you have control over the path your destiny will take?

Not someone else; not the circumstances around you; not even human nature. You, you have the power and you have the control.

And yes—you are destined for more!

This book is full of insights that build upon this concept: the path to your destiny is paved by you and your choice with these five traits.

In this book, we learn about the five traits that each of us possess and that each of us has the power to control—if we choose to be their master, rather than letting them be the masters of us.

Do you want to be in charge of your life, of your destiny, or do you want to be a circumstance, subservient to the whims of the world?

Our destiny that we desire could be the career we have dreamed about, it could be an award we have sacrificed and studied and practiced for, it could be the ultimate end goal for our life-the legacy we wish to leave behind when we are gone. It could be many things, but it will always lead to either death or life.

How we choose to accept or decline our power, our control, and our responsibility over these five traits, will greatly influence and determine the destiny we reach.

The five traits that are discussed in this book are not only unique to themselves, but they are intrinsically woven together to create the whole, the whole that has the ability and power to mold our destiny.

If you want to take control of your destiny, then read this book and grab the reins and make that choice.

Will you choose a destiny of life or death?

It is time we choose our destiny.

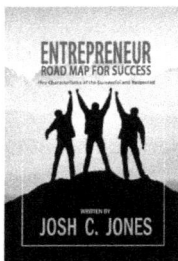

ENTREPRENEUR: Road Map For Success

Do you desire to be successful in your life?

Do you have a dream that you want to see become a reality?

Do you desire to build strong characteristics and to be respected in your life?

If the answer to these questions is yes, then You Absolutely Can!

The question is: Have you ever thought about being an entrepreneur?

Merriam-Webster states that an entrepreneur is "one who organizes, manages, and assumes the risk of a business or enterprise." This book, however, will reveal to you that an entrepreneur is much more than that—and that you, too, can be an entrepreneur.

This book breaks down the five characteristics that can greatly help lead you to success and respect in this world.

You can choose to incorporate and build these characteristics into your daily life— characteristics that will produce positive results, help you build your self-worth, achieve your dream, reach your success, and live a life worthy of respect.

Now is the time for you to be the entrepreneur for your life. Now is the time for you to achieve your success.

NOTES

NOTES

NOTES

NOTES